THE
IRISH REPUBLICANS' QUOTATION BOOK

THE
IRISH REPUBLICANS' QUOTATION BOOK

Compiled by Andrew Russell

SOMERVILLE PRESS

Somerville Press Ltd,
Dromore, Bantry, Co. Cork, Ireland

©Andrew Russell 2020

Designed by Jane Stark
Typeset in Minion Pro
seamistgraphics@gmail.com
ISBN: 978 1 9999970 90

Printed and bound in the EU

FRONT COVER PHOTO:
Michael Collins working the crowd in Dublin, 1922.
Wikimedia Commons
Photographer: Agency du Presse Meurisse;
Source: Bibliothèque Nationale de France

They haven't gone away you know.

Gerry Adams

> Making peace, I have found, is much harder than making war.
>
> *Gerry Adams*

> IF YOU MILITARIZE A SITUATION, YOU BEG FOR AN ARMED RESPONSE.
>
> *Gerry Adams*

> For over 30 years,
> the IRA showed that
> the British Government
> could not rule Ireland
> on its own terms.
>
> *Gerry Adams*

Parting is such a sad thing,
but we will meet one day
in heaven.
I will go to the gallows
as an Irishman
with love in my heart
for a free Ireland.

Kevin Barry

The freedom of Ireland is to me a second religion.

Brendan Behan

> THEY TOOK AWAY
> OUR LAND,
> AND OUR RELIGION:
> BUT THEY COULD
> NOT HARNESS
> OUR TONGUES.
>
> *Brendan Behan*

(*On killing Black and Tans*):

YES I KILLED THEM.
ALL KILLING IS MURDER TO ME.
I MAKE NO APOLOGIES
FOR KILLING
AND THE ONLY THING
I WAS REALLY SORRY FOR
WAS THE NUMBER THAT ESCAPED.

Dan Breen

> 'Come on, you cowards,
> 'till I get one shot before I die.
> I am only a wounded man.
> Éamonn, Éamonn (Ceannt).
> Come here and sing
> "God Save Ireland"
> before I die.'
>
> *Cathal Brugha*

Self-government is our right,

a thing born to us at birth,

a thing no more to be doled out

to us by another people

than the right to life itself,

or the right to feel the sun

or smell the flowers

or love our kind.

Sir Roger Casement

> I LEAVE FOR THE GUIDANCE
> OF OTHER REVOLUTIONARIES,
> WHO MAY TREAD THE PATH
> WHICH I HAVE TROD:
> NEVER TREAT WITH THE ENEMY,
> NEVER TO SURRENDER
> TO HIS MERCY,
> BUT TO FIGHT TO A FINISH.
>
> *Éamonn Ceannt*

(In a letter to his wife the night before his execution in 1916):

I am here without hope of this world, without fear, calmly awaiting the end. I die a noble death for Ireland's freedom. Be proud of me as I am and ever was of you.

Éamonn Ceannt

(*To his son*):

I WANT YOU TO SHAKE HANDS
WITH EVERY MINISTER IN THE
PROVISIONAL GOVERNMENT
WHO'S RESPONSIBLE
FOR MY DEATH.
I FORGIVE THEM
AND SO MUST YOU.

Erskine Childers

(*To the firing squad*):

Take a step or two forward lads... it will be easier that way.

Erskine Childers

I AND MY FELLOW SIGNATORIES
BELIEVE WE HAVE STRUCK
THE FIRST SUCCESSFUL BLOW
FOR IRISH FREEDOM.
THE NEXT BLOW,
WHICH WE HAVE NO DOUBT
IRELAND WILL STRIKE,
WILL WIN THROUGH.
IN THIS BELIEF, WE DIE HAPPY.

Tom Clarke

(*In a letter to his sister before his execution*):

May God help us – me to die well, you to bear your sorrow.

Con Colbert

There is no crime in detecting
and destroying in wartime
the spy and informer.
They have destroyed
without trial.
I have paid them back
in their own coin.

Michael Collins

Give us the future.
We have had enough
of the past.
Give us back
our country
to live in – to grow in.

Michael Collins

(After signing the Treaty):

THINK WHAT I HAVE GOT FOR IRELAND…
SOMETHING SHE HAS WANTED
THESE 700 YEARS.
WILL ANYONE BE SATISFIED
WITH THIS BARGAIN, WILL ANYONE?
I TELL YOU THIS, EARLY THIS MORNING
I HAVE SIGNED MY OWN DEATH WARRANT.

Michael Collins

(Just before leaving to face his fate in Beal na mBlath).

Yerra, they will never shoot me in my own county.

Michael Collins

THE IRISH PEOPLE
WILL BE FREE,
WHEN THEY OWN
EVERYTHING
FROM THE PLOUGH
TO THE STARS.

James Connolly

> IF YOU REMOVE THE ENGLISH ARMY TOMORROW AND HOIST THE GREEN FLAG OVER DUBLIN CASTLE, UNLESS YOU SET ABOUT THE ORGANIZATION OF THE SOCIALIST REPUBLIC, YOUR EFFORTS WOULD BE IN VAIN.
>
> *James Connolly*

THE IRISHMAN
IN ENGLISH LITERATURE
MAY BE SAID TO
HAVE BEEN BORN WITH
AN APOLOGY IN HIS MOUTH.

James Connolly

> We believe in constitutional action in normal times: we believe in revolutionary action in exceptional times.
>
> *James Connolly*

> As well you might
> leave the fairies
> to plough your land or
> the idle winds to sow it,
> as sit down
> and wait for freedom.
>
> *Thomas Davis*

> A PEOPLE WITHOUT
> A LANGUAGE
> OF ITS OWN
> IS ONLY
> HALF A NATION.
>
> *Thomas Davis*

It is not blood
that makes you Irish
but a willingness
to be part of
the Irish nation.

Thomas Davis

> It is my considered opinion that in the fullness of time history will record the greatness of Michael Collins and it will be recorded at my expense.
>
> *Éamon de Valera*

> Of course
> I wrote most of the
> Constitution
> myself.
>
> *Éamon de Valera*

I AM AGAINST THIS TREATY
NOT BECAUSE I AM
A MAN OF WAR
BUT BECAUSE I AM
A MAN OF PEACE.
I AM AGAINST THE TREATY
BECAUSE IT WILL NOT END
THE CENTURIES OF CONFLICT
BETWEEN THE TWO NATIONS OF
GREAT BRITAIN AND IRELAND.

Éamon de Valera

It wasn't long before
people discovered
the ultimate horror of
letting an urchin
into Parliament.

Bernadette Devlin

Even if I drift into a coma,
promise me that you won't
take me off the hunger strike
unless the five demands are met.
The British and Margaret
Thatcher won't break me
or my comrades.
We are not criminals, we are
Irish Political Prisoners of War,
and we will win in the end.

Kieran Doherty

What is peace? The kind that the Republican movement has been fighting for is peace with justice. Peace that our people can live, peace that our people can work and have houses, and that our people can walk free through the streets of their own towns, their own cities and their own country. It will be the peace that will be restored to the nation after 800 years when British imperialism leaves our shores.

Máire Drumm

(*In his speech from the dock
on the eve of his execution*):

LET THEM AND ME REPOSE IN PEACE,
AND MY TOMB REMAIN UNINSCRIBED,
UNTIL OTHER TIMES, AND OTHER MEN,
CAN DO JUSTICE TO MY CHARACTER;
WHEN MY COUNTRY TAKES HER PLACE
AMONG THE NATIONS OF THE EARTH,
THEN, ONLY THEN, LET MY EPITAPH
BE WRITTEN, I HAVE DONE.

Robert Emmet

I DON'T LIKE THIS
EXCLUSION OF WOMEN
FROM THE NATIONAL FIGHT,
AND THEY SHOULD HAVE
TO WORK THROUGH
BACK-DOOR INFLUENCE
TO GET THINGS DONE.

Maud Gonne

THE ENGLISH MAY
BATTER US TO PIECES,
BUT THEY WILL
NEVER SUCCEED IN
BREAKING OUR SPIRIT.

Maud Gonne

So far as
my power extends,
not one single
Irish life will be lost
in that quibble.

Arthur Griffith

> Strange people,
> alien to us in thought,
> alien to us in sympathy,
> who came to
> live among us
> but never became
> one of us.
>
> *Arthur Griffith*

I HAVE NO PROUDER BOAST
THAN TO SAY I AM IRISH
AND HAVE BEEN PRIVILEGED TO FIGHT
FOR THE IRISH PEOPLE AND IRELAND.
IF I HAVE A DUTY I WILL PERFORM IT TO
THE FULL WITH THE UNSHAKABLE BELIEF
THAT WE ARE A NOBLE RACE
AND THAT CHAINS AND BOUNDS
HAVE NO PART IN US.

Francis Hughes

> As our language
> wanes and dies,
> the golden legends
> of the far-off centuries
> fade and pass away.
>
> *Douglas Hyde*

Oh, Irishmen, forget the past,
Whack fol the diddle fol the di dol day
And think of the day that is coming fast,
Whack fol the diddle fol the di dol day
When we shall all be civilized,
Neat and clean and well advised.
Oh, won't Mother England be surprised!
Whack fol the diddle fol the di dol day

Peadar Kearney

> INTOLERANCE
> HAS BEEN
> THE CURSE
> OF OUR COUNTRY.
>
> *James Larkin*

No, men and women
of the Irish race,
we will not fight for England.
We shall fight for
the destruction of
the British Empire
and the construction
of an Irish Republic.

James Larkin

(*As he stood before the firing squad*):

FIRE AWAY.
I HAVE BEEN LOOKING DOWN
THE BARRELS OF RIFLES
ALL MY LIFE.

John McBride

(Before his execution)

I FEEL HAPPINESS
THE LIKE OF WHICH
I HAVE NEVER EXPERIENCED.
I DIE THAT THE IRISH NATION
MIGHT LIVE.

Sean McDermott

> "The greatest glory
> you shall see
> And the greater peace
> beyond these wars."
>
> *Thomas McDonagh*

It seems to me the that
(the Irish Government)
were quite prepared
to throw the peace process
under a bus for the sake of
a few points in an opinion poll
– that is a disgraceful approach.

Mary-Lou McDonald

> I AM FULLY AWARE OF
> THE PAIN AND SUFFERING
> I WILL HAVE TO ENDURE
> AND I KNOW THAT IN THE END
> I MAY AND MOST LIKELY WILL
> HAVE TO FORFEIT MY LIFE.
>
> *Tom McElwee*

There are
no military solutions –
dialogue and diplomacy
are the only guarantee
of lasting peace.

Martin McGuinness

I was proud to be
a member of the IRA.
I am still 40 years on proud that
I was a member of the IRA.
I am not going to be a hypocrite
and sit here and
say something different.

Martin McGuinness

I NEVER TALK ABOUT
SHOOTING ANYBODY,
BUT I DO ACKNOWLEDGE THAT
I WAS A MEMBER OF THE IRA,
AND AS A MEMBER OF THE IRA,
I OBVIOUSLY ENGAGED
IN FIGHTING BACK
AGAINST THE BRITISH ARMY.

Martin McGuinness

> IF I DIE I KNOW
> THE FRUIT WILL EXCEED
> THE COST A THOUSAND FOLD.
> THE THOUGHT OF IT
> MAKES ME HAPPY.
> I THANK GOD FOR IT.
>
> *Terence McSwiney*

A Prayer,
written while he was in prison in July 1916.

Because I have endured the pain

Of waiting when my comrades die

Let me be swept in war's red rain

And friends and foes be justified.

Terence McSwiney

> Dress suitably
> in short skirts
> and sitting boots,
> leave your jewels
> in the bank
> and buy a revolver.
>
> *Countess Markiewicz*

While Ireland is not free
I remain a rebel,
unconverted and unconvertible.
There is no word
strong enough for it.
I am pledged as a rebel,
an unconvertible rebel,
to the one thing –
a free and independent Republic.

Countess Markiewicz

No man is as anti-feminist as a really feminist woman.

Countess Markiewicz

I HAVE ALWAYS HATED WAR
AND AM BY NATURE A PACIFIST
BUT IT IS THE ENGLISH
WHO ARE FORCING WAR ON US,
AND THE FIRST PRINCIPLE OF
WAR IS TO KILL THE ENEMY.

Countess Markiewicz

GENTLEMEN,
YOU MAY SOON HAVE
THE ALTERNATIVE TO
LIVE AS SLAVES OR
DIE AS FREE MEN.

Daniel O'Connell

THE POOR OLD
DUKE (OF WELLINGTON)!
WHAT SHALL I SAY OF HIM?
TO BE SURE
HE WAS BORN IN IRELAND,
BUT BEING BORN IN A STABLE
DOES NOT MAKE A MAN A HORSE.

Daniel O'Connell

THE ALTAR OF LIBERTY
TOTTERS WHEN
IT IS CEMENTED
ONLY WITH BLOOD.

Daniel O'Connell

There can be no such thing as an
Irish nationalist accepting the
Loyalist veto and partition.
You cannot claim to be an
Irish nationalist if you consent to
an internal six county settlement
and if you are willing to negotiate
the state of Irish society
with a foreign government.

Patsy O'Hara

> It is in that English Parliament
> that chains for Ireland
> are forged,
> and any Irish patriot into
> that forge to free Ireland
> will soon find himself welded
> into the agency of his
> country's subjection to England.
>
> *Jeremiah O'Donovan Rossa*

> I WILL ALWAYS REMEMBER AND COMMEMORATE OUR PATRIOT DEAD – AND EACH OF OUR FALLEN COMRADES WHO GAVE THEIR LIVES FOR IRISH FREEDOM.
>
> *Michelle O'Neill*

Why should Ireland
be treated as
a geographical fragment
of England –
Ireland is not a
geographical fragment,
but a nation.

Charles Stewart Parnell

No man has the right
to fix the boundary
of the march
of a nation:
no man has the right
to say to his country –
thus far shalt thou go
and no further.

Charles Stewart Parnell

Ireland unfree shall never be at peace.

Patrick Pearse

You cannot conquer Ireland;
you cannot extinguish
the Irish passion for freedom.
If our deed has not been
sufficient to win freedom,
then our children
will win it by a better deed.

Patrick Pearse

> A COUNTRY WITHOUT A LANGUAGE IS A COUNTRY WITHOUT A SOUL.
>
> *Patrick Pearse*

> We are ready to die
> and shall die
> cheerfully and proudly,
> you must not grieve
> for all of this.
>
> *Patrick Pearse*

Fraud, robbery and murder

have characterized

the English usurpation

of our country.

John Redmond

I AM A POLITICAL PRISONER BECAUSE I AM A CASUALTY OF A PERENNIAL WAR THAT IS BEING FOUGHT BY THE OPPRESSED IRISH PEOPLE AND AN ALIEN, OPPRESSIVE UNWANTED REGIME THAT REFUSES TO WITHDRAW FROM OUR LAND.

Bobby Sands

They won't break me because of the desire for freedom, and the freedom of the Irish people is in my heart. The day will dawn when all the people of Ireland will have the desire for freedom to show. It is then that we will see the rising of the moon.

Bobby Sands

Our revenge will be the laughter of our children.

Bobby Sands

> Until the women of Ireland are free, the men will not achieve emancipation.
>
> *Hanna Sheehy-Skeffington*

> Many suffer
> so that some day
> all Irish people
> may know
> justice and peace.
>
> *Wolfe Tone*

I HAVE SACRIFICED
FOR THE REPUBLIC
ALL THAT MAN HOLDS DEAR:
MY WIFE, MY CHILDREN,
MY LIBERTY AND MY LIFE.

Wolfe Tone

AFTER ALL I HAVE DONE
FOR A SACRED CAUSE,
DEATH IS NO SACRIFICE.

Wolfe Tone

Weary Men, what reap ye?
Golden corn for the stranger.
What sow ye? Human corpses
that wait for the avenger.
Fainting forms, hunger stricken,
what see you in the offing?
Stately ships to bear our food away,
amid the stranger's scoffing.
There's a proud array of soldiers –
what do they round your door?
They guard our master's granaries
from the thin hands of the poor.
Pale mothers, wherefore weeping? –
Would to God that we were dead
Our children swoon before us,
and we cannot give them bread.

Jane Wilde

For England may keep faith
For all that is done and said.
We know their dream; enough
To know they dreamed and are dead;
And what if excess of love
Bewildered them till they died?
I write it out in verse –
McDonagh and McBride
And Connolly and Pearse
Now and in time to be,
Wherever green is worn,
Are changed, changed utterly
A terrible beauty is born.

William Butler Yeats

IRISH WRITERS' INDEX

Gerry Adams (1948 -) Leader of Sinn Féin from 1983 to 2018. Elected TD for Louth in 2011 ...5

Kevin Barry (1902-1920) Medical student and IRA volunteer. Aged 18, he was hanged in Mounjoy Prison for the killing of a British soldier ...9

Brendan Behan (1923-1964) Poet, novelist, playwright and IRA Volunteer ...10

Dan Breen (1894-1969) IRA Volunteer and later Fianna Fáil TD ...12

Cathal Brugha (1874-1922) Chief of Staff of the IRA 1917-1919. President of Dáil Éireann January to April 1919 ...13

Sir Roger Casement (1864-1916) British diplomat and Irish nationalist. Executed in London for his part in the Easter Rising 14

Éamonn Ceannt (1881-1916) Member of the Irish Republican Brotherhood and one of the seven signatories of the Proclamation of Independence 15

Erskine Childers (1870-1922) Author and Irish Republican, born in London of an English father and Irish mother. Executed by the authorities of the Irish Free State for his part in the Civil War 17

Tom Clarke (1858-1916) Member of the Irish Republican Brotherhood and the first and oldest of the signatories of the Proclamation of Independence 19

Con Colbert (1888-1916) Irish Volunteer and pioneer of Fianna Éireann.................20

Michael Collins (1890-1922) Revolutionary, soldier and politician. He was Chairman of the Provisional Government of the Irish Free State from January 1922 until he was shot dead in an ambush by anti-treaty forces in August 1922 21

James Connolly (1868-1916) Scottish-born Irish Republican and socialist leader. Member of the Irish Socialist Republican Party and with James Larkin formed the Irish Citizen Army 25

Thomas Davis (1814-1845) Writer and chief organiser of the Young Ireland movement. Famous nationalistic ballads included 'The West's Asleep' and 'A Nation Once Again' ...29

Éamonn De Valera (1882-1975) Having been sentenced to death for his part in the Easter Rising, he was released and became one of the leaders of the War of Independence. He served as Taoiseach on three different occasions and was President of Ireland from 1959 to 1973.. 32

Bernadette Devlin (1947-) Irish civil rights leader and former politician. In 1969, at the age of 21, she was elected as MP for Mid Ulster and served until 1974.........................35

Kieran Doherty (1955-1981) Hunger striker, volunteer in the Belfast Brigade of the Provisional IRA and briefly TD for Cavan-Monaghan. He lasted 73 days on hunger strike 36

Máire Drumm (1919-1976) Vice President of Sinn Féin and a commander in Cumann na mBan. She was twice jailed for making seditious speeches and was eventually shot dead in her hospital bed by loyalist paramilitaries...........................37

Robert Emmet (1778-1803) Irish Republican, orator and rebel leader. At the age of 25 he led an abortive rebellion against British rule. He was captured, tried and executed for high treason 38

Maud Gonne (McBride) (1866-1953) English-born Irish revolutionary, suffragette and actress. Of Anglo-Irish descent, she was won over to Irish nationalism by the plight of evicted people in the Land Wars 39

Arthur Griffith (1871-1922) Writer and politician, who founded Sinn Féin and was leader of the Irish delegation that produced the 1921 Anglo-Irish Treaty. He served as President of Dáil Éireann during the last year of his life 41

Francis Hughes (1956-1981) Volunteer in the Provisional IRA and hunger striker. Until his arrest he was the most wanted man in Northern Ireland. He lasted 59 days on hunger strike . . 43

Douglas Hyde (1860-1949) Irish academic, Irish language scholar and politician. He was the first President of Ireland, serving from 1938 to 1945, and the first President of the Gaelic League. . 44

Peadar Kearney (1883-1942) Irish republican and composer of numerous rebel songs, including 'A Soldiers Song', now the National Anthem. He was also the uncle of Brendan and Dominic Behan. 45

James Larkin (1876-1947) Liverpool-born Irish republican, socialist and trade union leader. He was one of the founders of the Irish Citizen Army, the Irish Labour Party and the Workers' Union of Ireland. He serves as a TD on three separate occasions. 46

John McBride (1868-1916) Irish republican and military leader who was executed for his part in the Easter Rising. He was the husband of Maud Gonne and father of Sean McBride 48

Sean McDermott (1883-1916) Irish republican political activist and revolutionary leader. He was one of seven leaders of the Easter Rising and a signatory of the Proclamation of the Irish Republic 49

Thomas MacDonagh (1878-1916) Political

activist, poet, playwright and revolutionary leader. He was one of the seven leaders of the Easter Rising and a signatory of the Proclamation of the Irish Republic. He was commemorated in several poems by W.B Yeats.................................50

Mary-Lou McDonald (1969-) Sinn Féin politician who became President of the party in February 2018. She was formerly Vice President of Sinn Féin , and was also a member of the European Parliament for five years..................51

Thomas McElwee (1957-1981) Provisional IRA volunteer and hunger striker. He died at the age of 23 after a 62 day hunger strike...........52

Martin McGuinness (1950-2017) Deputy First Minister of Northern Ireland 2007-2017, he was formerly a member of the Provisional IRA. He was one of the main architects of the Good Friday Agreement........................53

Terence McSwiney (1879-1920) Playwright, author and poliician. When serving as Lord Mayor of Cork, he was arrested on charges of sedition and imprisoned in Brixton Prison. He died there after a 74 day hunger strike 56

Countess Markiewicz (1868-1927) Politician, revolutionary and suffragette, she was the first woman elected to the Westminster Parliament...........................58

Daniel O'Connell (1775-1847) Known as The Liberator, he was an Irish political leader during the first half of the nineteenth century. He campaigned for Catholic Emancipation and the repeal of the Act of Union between Great Britain and Ireland. 62

Patsy O'Hara (1957-1981) Hunger Striker and member of the INLA. Died at the age of 23 after a hunger strike lasting 61 days. 65

Jeremiah O'Donovan Rossa (1831-1915) Irish Fenian leader and prominent member of the Irish Republican Brotherhood 66

Michelle O'Neill (1977-) Northern Irish politician, who was appointed vice-president of Sinn Féin in 2018 and deputy First Minister of Northern Ireland in 2020 67

Charles Stewart Parnell (1846-1891) Nationalist politician who serves as Leader of the Irish Parliamentary Party from 1882 to 1891 and leader of the Home Rule League from 1880 to

1882. Westminster MP from 1875 to 1891...68

Patrick Pearse (1879-1916) Irish language teacher, republican political activist and revolutionary. Following his execution, he was seen by many to be the embodiment of the rebellion 70

John Redmond (1856-1918) Nationalist politician, barrister and MP in the British House of Commons. Leader of the moderate Irish Parliamentary Party (IPP) from 1900 to 1918....................................74

Bobby Sands (1954-1981) Leader of the 1981 hunger strike in the Maze prison, where he was imprisoned for firearms offences. During the strike he was elected as MP for Fermanagh and South Tyrone. He died after 66 days of his hunger strike 75

Hanna Sheehy-Skeffington (1877-1946) Suffragette and Irish nationalist. She was one of the founders of the Irish Women's Franchise League and the Irish Women Workers' Union 78

Theobald Wolfe Tone (1763-1798) Leading Irish revolutionary and one of the founding members of the United Irishmen. He is generally regarded as the father of Irish republicanism. After his capture during the 1798 Rebellion, he was sentenced to be hanged in Dublin. Before the sentence could be carried out he died of wounds sustained in prison. . .79

Jane Wilde (1821-1896) Poet, who sometimes wrote under the pen name 'Speranza', and Irish nationalist. Oscar Wilde was her younger son 82

W.B. Yeats (1865-1939) Poet and one of the foremost literary figures of the twentieth century. He served two terms as a Senator of the Irish Free State 83